SEX
AND THE
NEW YOU

Richard Bimler

**For ages
11 to 14
and
parents**

Book 4 of the Learning about Sex Series

The titles in the series:

Unless otherwise indicated, Scripture quotations are from the Revised Standard Version of the Bible, copyrighted 1946, 1952, © 1971, 1973. Used by permission.

Scripture quotations marked TEV are from the Good News Bible, the Bible in TODAYS ENGLISH VERSION. Copyright © American Bible Society 1966, 1971, 1976. Used by permission.

Scripture quotations marked NEB are from THE NEW ENGLISH BIBLE (NEB) © The Delegates of the Oxford University Press and the Syndics of the Cambridge University Press, 1961, 1970, and are used by permission.

Developed under the auspices of the Family Life Department
Board for Parish Services
The Lutheran Church—Missouri Synod

Illustrations by Maritz Communications Company. Cover design by Concordia Publishing House.

Copyright © 1982, 1988, 1995
Concordia Publishing House
3558 South Jefferson Avenue
Saint Louis, Missouri 63118-3968

Manufactured in the United States of America

1 2 3 4 5 6 7 8 9 10   04 03 02 01 00 99 98 97 96 95

Contents

Editor's Foreword

This book is one of a series of six published under the auspices of the Board for Parish Services of The Lutheran Church—Missouri Synod through its family life department.

Originally published in 1982, the series was updated in 1988, and again in 1995. This 1995 update includes topics of concern that have emerged since 1988.

Books in the series are *Why Boys and Girls Are Different* (Ages 3–5); *Where Do Babies Come From?* (Ages 6–8); *How You Are Changing* (Ages 8–11); *Sex and the New You* (Ages 11–14); *Love, Sex, and God* (Ages 14+); and *How to Talk Confidently with Your Child about Sex ... and Appreciate Your Own Sexuality Too.*

The last book in the series is designed for adults, to help them deal with their own sexuality, as well as to provide practical assistance for married and single parents in their role as sex educators in the home.

Sex and the New You is the fourth book in the series. It is written especially for young people (ages 11 to 14) and, of course, for the parents, teachers, and other concerned grownups who may want to discuss the book with them.

Like its predecessor, the new *Learning about Sex* series provides information about the social-psychological and physiological aspects of human sexuality. But more: it does so from a distinctively Christian point of view, in the context of our relationship to the God who created us and redeemed us in Jesus Christ.

The series presents sex as another good gift from God which is to be used responsibly.

Each book in the series is graded—in vocabulary and in the amount of information it provides. It answers the questions that persons at each age level typically ask.

Because children vary widely in their growth rates and interest levels, parents and other concerned adults will want to preview each book in the series, directing the child to the next graded book when he or she is ready for it.

In addition to reading each book, you can use them as starting points for casual conversation, and when answering other questions a child might have.

This book can also be used as a mini-unit or as part of another course of study in a Christian school setting. (Correlated video and study resources are available for both curricular and home use.) Whenever the book is used in a class setting, it is important to let the parents know beforehand, since they have the prime responsibility for the sex education of their children.

While parents will appreciate the help of the school, they will want to know what is being taught. As the Christian home and the Christian school work together, Christian values in sex education can be more effectively strengthened.

Frederick J. Hofmeister, M.D., FACOG, Wawatosa, Wisconsin, served as medical adviser for the series.

Rev. Ronald W. Brusius, secretary of family life education, Board for Parish Services, served as chief subject-matter consultant.

In addition to the staffs of the Board for Parish Services and Concordia Publishing House, the following special consultants helped conceptualize the series: Darlene Armbruster, board member, National Lutheran Parent-Teacher League; Betty Brusius, executive director, National Lutheran Parent-Teacher League; Margaret Gaulke, elementary school guidance counselor; Priscilla Henkelman, early childhood specialist; Rev. Lee Hovel, youth specialist; Robert G. Miles, Lutheran Child and Family Service of Michigan; Margaret Noettl, family life specialist; and Bonnie Schlechte, lecturer on teen sexuality.

Rev. Earl H. Gaulke, Ph.D.

1. You've Heard and You've Wondered

"How does a girl get pregnant?"

"What's a 'wet dream'?"

"Will my breasts ever develop?"

"What is a homosexual?"

"What size should a penis be?"

"Am I normal?"

You've heard questions like these before—maybe you've asked them yourself. And maybe you haven't been quite sure about the answers.

This book won't tell you everything you ever wanted to know about sex, but it will help you understand a bit more and give you answers to some of the questions you have about your body, about getting along with others, and about the whole fascinating world of sex and sexuality.

More importantly, this book won't ever let you forget who gave you life and made you what you are. You are a child of God. Because God cared enough, He sent His very best, His own Son, to live and die for you. This kind of love means He won't ever ignore you; He'll guide you and protect you and forgive you. Because Christ died for you and paid the penalty for your sins, God is able to accept you just as you are. And because Christ became a human being, He understands your questions about sex, your wonderings about your body, and your sexual daydreaming. He helps you to grow in a healthy relationship with Him, with other people, and with yourself.

He helps you to become a "New You."

Of course, reading this book won't automatically solve all your problems. You may still be disappointed with your body, the way you look, the way you feel. But you will have the chance to look honestly at these things and to think and talk about them. You may wish you were different, but you will hear again and again that you were made by God.

Below are a few more of the questions that people your age ask. On the next page is some space for writing in your own questions that aren't included. Take a moment now to write them in if you want to. Then, when you've finished the book, come back to see whether they have been answered.

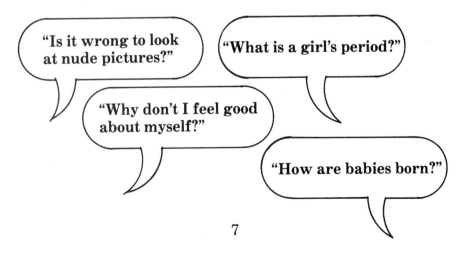

"Is it wrong to look at nude pictures?"

"What is a girl's period?"

"Why don't I feel good about myself?"

"How are babies born?"

Questions I Wonder About

_____

_____

_____

_____

_____

_____

_____

2. You're Someone Special!

He: "Sometimes I think God made me
to be weird and dumb!"

She: "Why do you say that?"

He: "Because I'm always messing things up. I don't do
anything right. Do you ever feel that way?"

She: "Sure, lots of times. And I think everybody feels that
way sometime."

He: "Are you kidding? . . . That's just my luck. I just found
the second person in the world who is weird and dumb!"

"Am I normal?" ask many young people. It's so easy to feel
alone and different. It's easy to think that you are the only
person feeling the way you do—about your body, your family,
your self. Maybe you feel this way because of the changes in your
body and your increased sexual desires. You may feel this way
because your body is not growing as rapidly as other people
around you. Or perhaps your body is way ahead of the pack, and
that doesn't feel so good either.

It's good to have a friend you can talk with when you're not feeling good about yourself. But it's especially great to have Jesus as our Friend! He can actually "feel sympathy for our weaknesses," the Bible reminds us, because He "was tempted in every way that we are but did not sin" (Hebrews 4:15-16 TEV). He really *knows* how we feel, because He was born and grew and went through the teen years too. That's why we can talk to Him and know He'll understand.

Even more, as your Savior, He can really help! He lived and died and rose again to make you a child of the heavenly Father. He's living proof that the "Father Himself loves you." That's good to remember when you're feeling unlovable or guilty or anxious or scared.

The God who loves you and forgives you is the same God who made you. No one else—not even your "identical" twin, is exactly like you. You are special; no carbon copy or clone of someone else. You look different, you feel different, you think differently from anyone else. You grow at a different rate, maybe in spurts, maybe at a fairly regular pace. But whatever your "growth pattern," it's just right for you—because God made you and set your pattern into motion. When you accept that, you can accept a lot of the other things about yourself.

So don't quit on yourself! Don't give up hope and quit trying. Perhaps you won't ever be the glamorous model or towering athlete you wish you could be, but you can do a lot with what you've got. Once you accept yourself as you are and decide you're worth taking care of, ask yourself the following questions. The answers you give will suggest what you can do to take care of your body—and your feelings about yourself.

1. How much sleep do I get each night? Do I sometimes harm my body with a lack of rest and sleep? How can I improve on this?

2. What are my eating habits? Do they hinder the growth of my body or help it? Am I a "junk food" addict or do I eat good, solid, nourishing food? Do I have a tendency to eat too little or too much? What can I do to help my body by changing some of my eating habits?

3. Are some of my complexion problems due to the sweets and other "empty" calories I eat? And do I wash often enough to keep my skin from being too greasy and oily? Should I seek the advice of my doctor?

4. What about exercise? Is my body mistreated with too much jogging and too much exertion? Or do I get most of my

exercise sharpening my pencil or falling out of bed?

5. What are my feelings about smoking? Do I see it as a "neat" thing to do, to be one of the group? Or do I take seriously the studies that show the harm and danger in smoking? Am I one of the statistics that reveal that teenage smoking is on the increase, especially among girls, even though it is a fact that smoking is harmful to you—and to those around you?

6. And what about drugs? And alcohol? Do I abuse my body by taking drugs and drinking alcohol?

Even if your answers show that you sometimes misuse your body and don't show the concern about it you might, God is concerned. After all, He formed your body and programmed it to work in a certain way, and He gave you common sense to take care of it. Sure, you forget now and then, but He doesn't. Remember, He's got quite an investment in you. "You are not your own; you were bought with a price. So glorify God in your body," writes St. Paul (1 Corinthians 6:19-20).

Even if your complexion is poor right now, even if you're a bit overweight, even if you're carrying a physical handicap every step of the way—you are His, and He's proud of that. Peek in the mirror again; go ahead, it won't hurt. Look beyond the familiar surface and find the hand of God there. See if you don't feel a little different now—maybe even a little proud.

3. Sex Is More Than Body Parts

She: "What's the difference between sex and sexuality?"

He: "Is this some kind of a game or something? I don't know, and what's more, I don't even care!"

She: "Let me ask you a question: Are you the opposite sex, or am I?"

He: "Why don't you go talk to somebody else for a while!"

People can get very confused about the word "sex." Basically, "sex" refers to the physical characteristics that make men different from women. Many people use "sex" to refer to the act of intercourse or to physical attraction between men and women, but technically it means only the simple physical description and labeling of body parts.

For Christians, however, sex means more than just body parts. It's how we feel about and use our body parts as *good gifts of God.* Take, for example, the mother who was making sure that her six-year-old son was washing properly. "Be sure to wash your ears and your face and your hands—and your penis, too," she said.

As a Christian mother, she knew that a penis is as good a creation of God as is a hand or face. There's no need to feel embarrassed about our body parts. And certainly there's no reason to consider any part of our body as "dirty" or not to be mentioned.

Obviously, even a child who knows the proper names for those parts needs to learn common sense about when and where to use the names. Lots of people use nicknames for "penis" or "vagina" in vulgar stories or jokes. But that doesn't mean these parts are "dirty." How could anything God made be dirty? Thanking God for your body includes thanking Him for your penis or vagina or breasts as well as for your eyes and ears.

When God first created people, He made them perfect. That means their *bodies* were perfect and *VERY GOOD*—every part of their bodies. God Himself said all His creation was "good." Take a moment now to look at your hand. Open and close your fingers—slowly. Clinch your fingers in a tight fist. Ask yourself: What man-made machine can move with such precision—instantly—simply on the command of your mind? What machine can be so gentle and yet so strong as a human hand? Picture the marvelous things that hands can do: hands moving over a keyboard, playing an intricate composition; a surgeon's hands, skillfully manipulating instruments in open-heart surgery; a mother's hands, gently stroking her baby's fevered face.

Think of your eye—more wonderful than a camera. It sees color, motion; adjusts itself to dim light or bright sun; focuses automatically; never needs film; develops its pictures instantly.

As we'll see in a later chapter, your sex organs are just as wonderfully made as your hand or your eye. For God Himself "arranged the organs in the body, each one of them, as He chose" (1 Corinthians 12:18).

4. Is Sex a Secret?

John: "Look at all the sex around—movies, TV, songs, ads, jokes—it's everywhere!"

Mary: "Yes, except in the home."

John: "What do you mean?"

Mary: "I mean we seldom talk about it in my home. Do you?"

John: "Not really."

Mary: "Well, why don't *you* ask your dad about it?"

John: "No way! Sorry I brought it up!"

A lot of people never talk about sex; some think it's wrong to use the word. Even a lot of parents feel uncomfortable talking to their children about sex and reproduction. Whether such talk is easy or difficult in your home depends a lot on the way your parents were raised. Those raised in homes where sex was a secret often have trouble talking about sex and sexuality even when they know they want to share their thoughts and feelings.

14

If you sense this hesitation in your home, you might be able to make the situation a little easier for your parents. Since they find it difficult to bring up the subject, you can help by asking some of the questions you have in a serious, mature way. You might share books like this one with them and together explore those subjects that concern you most. You'll find most parents quite willing to talk once their first embarrassment has worn off.

Try making a list of questions that you'd like to ask your parents and find a time to ask them when nothing else is interfering. Don't dump all of them at once; try one and see if that doesn't break the ice. You have a real chance to show your parents you are growing up and that you want to talk to them in a mature way. It's a good way to improve communications in your family and to help the family grow together. If it doesn't work at first, the idea will have been planted; the next time they may be more ready.

Parents aren't the only ones you can get information from. You probably know other adults—a pastor, counselor, teacher, relative, or neighbor—whom you like and who might be willing to listen to your questions. Sometimes friends can be helpful, but often they're hard to talk to because you don't want them to think you're "out of it" when you have such questions. Even those friends who seem to talk most freely about sex may be giving you more imagination than facts, and you want facts.

Obviously there's a lot of talk about sex in school, but so much of it gives sex the bad name that many feel it has. Slang terms, dirty jokes, and laughter of a certain kind are often ways that people use to cover their own embarrassment, lack of information, and misconceptions about sex. Such activity cheapens God's wonderful gift and increases the misunderstandings that cause most of the problems young people feel.

Sex shouldn't be a secret. You can help break the wall of silence by asking questions of those who know the answers and are willing to talk, by treating sexual terminology and attitudes with respect, and by thanking God for making you who and what you are. Pretending sex doesn't exist or keeping information about it a secret will only prolong the ignorance and add to the confusion.

5. You're Changing into a New You

She: "Why am I taller than you?"
He: "Who knows? I don't think I'll ever get any higher than 2'6"."
She: "Oh, come on. You must be at least 3'5" by now!"
He: "You're such a big help! At least I'm 'down to earth.' How is the weather way up there, anyway?"

You probably don't need the title of this chapter to know that its words are true. You probably knew something was different when the bottoms of your jeans no longer touched the ground. Or when you had trouble not tripping as you walked across a level floor. Or maybe when your moments of depression or frustration increased. No, you probably don't need a book to tell you that you're changing; you see it, feel it, sense it all the time.

It's called "adolescence," and when adults use the word they may shake their heads and raise their eyebrows at the same time. Adolescence is the age of "becoming," of changing from a child into an adult. It is a very necessary trip, and often it will be an exciting trip for you. But it will also be frustrating both to you and to others, mostly because of the changes going on in you and your concerns about them. Since joys and frustrations are both part of adolescence, you might as well look forward to them and accept them.

Your body is changing and so is your personality. You feel more strongly about big things and little things. You want to be more involved in decisions. You want to be on your own to try out some new ideas, to do some new things. It's all part of "growing up." At times, you'll feel pulled in both directions; half the time you'll want the freedoms of the adult, and half the time you'll want the security of the child. And there's not a lot you can do about it. Just try to accept it. You won't be the only one with feelings like these.

The best thing you can do is remember who you are. God made you, and He accepts you at each stage of your growing. You are special to Him, and He'll guide you along this path too. Use this time to discover who you are and to develop your own style, your personality, and respect the body you've been given. Be what you are—in Him!

As you work at finding out what and who you are, you're going to look around at others. You'll see some who are like you want to be and a lot who aren't. Use these models to shape your actions, but don't lose yourself in the process. Heroes and models are fine, but remember that you are *you* and most of what you're going to be will come from inside you, not from anyone else.

It's so easy to assume that popularity depends on what you *are*, but you'll find more often that it's based on how you treat, respect, and act toward others. Be yourself, without ever forgetting that others are important too. God has given you a lot. Your happiness will depend on how well you use those gifts and how comfortable you are with them.

Your Body Is Changing

Most of us have a time in our life when we grow very rapidly, our "growth spurt." Some of you may already have begun; some may still be waiting. You don't need to worry if it hasn't hit you yet; it will. You'll almost be able to see your legs stretch out. You'll outgrow your clothes before you wear them out.

17

Most girls enter this stage between 9 and 12; boys are usually later, usually between 12 and 14. It's not at all unusual for girls to be taller than boys during the junior high years. It might be a little embarrassing or awkward that this happens just when boys and girls start noticing each other, but usually by age 15 boys catch up and pass most girls.

You'll become much more aware of your height and weight during these years. You'll measure, weigh, compare with others frequently, and you'll probably be concerned when you don't seem to be growing as fast as others or when others aren't growing as fast as you are. Differences in growth rate are common—and normal.

Few of you will be exactly the size you'd like to be; most of you will be larger than your parent of the same sex, but not all. Some of you boys are on the way to being 6'5" or more, and some of you girls will probably reach 6 feet. But not all will. Some of you will have to "watch your weight" all your lives; others will seem never to gain. Most boys will gain 12—20 pounds a year at age 14 or 15, after that maybe 6 or 8 pounds a year. And the girls, who gained earlier, will add only 5 or 6 pounds a year by the time they're 15. Sure, heredity has a lot to do with it, but so does what and how you eat.

The main thing to remember is that differences are normal—and good. Imagine a world where all of us matured at exactly the same rate and wound up exactly the same size and shape. What a bore! God knew what He was doing when He made each of you different. Where would basketball be if everyone could "dunk" or where no one could? Where would that sport be without the quick little guards darting between the big guys? And where would it be without all those who participate in the game only as spectators?

There's a place for everyone and a role for everyone. Try them all until you find the one that fits best; then accept it and become the best you can in that role.

One of the changes you'll be most concerned about is the way you look. Your face is changing just like the rest of your body. Your mouth, nose, chin are all starting to look more like an adult's than like a child's. You're not going to grow an extra eye or ear or anything spectacular, but you'll see differences when you compare your grade school pictures with what you see in the mirror.

And that mirror is going to concern you lots of times. Sometimes you're not going to like the way your hair looks. And you're probably going to spend a lot of time trying to make it

look like someone else's. That might work, at least until the first gust of wind. But your biggest concern in the mirror is sure to be your complexion.

Most of you will go through a time when acne—blackheads or pimples or something more bothersome—will affect your complexion. Some of you will have real problems with acne. If basic facial cleanliness and standard acne treatments don't seem to be controlling it, talk to your doctor about it. Acne won't cause you a lot of joy, but people do understand the common condition, and it usually passes by the time you're 18 or 19.

Growing Sexually

The pituitary gland, located at the bottom of your brain, has been regulating most of the growth changes taking place in your body. This gland has also caused your sexual glands to mature, and as they mature, growth usually slows down as sexual maturity is reached. The product of these glands is called a "hormone," and these hormones cause a number of changes in your bodies, especially those which distinguish boys from girls.

If you are a girl, you will notice that your hips become wider and your breasts begin to grow, perhaps as early as the age of 10

pituitary gland

or 11. Hair will begin to grow under your arms and in your pubic area. Your voice will mature and become richer and fuller.

If you are a boy, you will experience these changes sometime between the ages of 12 and 17. Your chest will expand. your shoulders become wider, and hair will appear under your arms, on your chest, on your face, and in your pubic area. Your voice, too, will change, but not as easily as does a girl's. Most of you will find that, as your voice changes when you are about 14 or 15, it will crack and squeak without warning until the change is complete. Most of you will begin to shave by age 16, something you'll continue through most of your lives.

Remember, these changes will occur at different times and in different ways. You may be maturing faster than most of those around you, or you may appear to be standing still. But you *are* changing, even if you can't see it or feel it yet.

At times you're sure to get depressed about all this, and there will be moments when others just can't seem to understand your moods and feelings. Even when your friends and parents get impatient, God understands. He's watching and He's in control. His love continues even when you and everyone else and the whole world are changing.

Remember

You may feel like a stranger to yourself and not at all sure what is happening;

You may feel embarrassed talking to others, even those your own age, especially if they're developing at a different rate than you are;

You may feel out of place if you haven't developed as much as some of your friends;

You might have trouble being honest about your own feelings, even to yourself;

You might feel pressure to conform to what others expect of you and to look and act like everyone else, even when you don't want to,

You might find yourself wanting to be alone more than ever before;

You might be trying to act more grown up than you really are;

You might find yourself thinking more about those of the other sex, even dreaming or fantasizing about sex. You might be feeling guilty about these thoughts and the feelings that go along with them.

None of these thoughts and feelings are unusual, nor are they abnormal. They are very much a part of growing up, a very natural part of learning to adjust to a "new body." Some of them show you need assurance, others show you need information. The chapters that follow in this book hope to provide both. As you prepare to read and discuss them, you might find it helpful to review or to add to the questions you've already jotted down in Chapter 1. You may want to share the questions with someone close, or you may just wish to keep them for yourself as you read the following chapters.

And as you walk the journey through this stage, remember that

• God loves you, just the way you are;

• you need to learn to respect yourself (and your body) before you can start respecting other people (and their bodies);

• your parents, and other adults, made it through adolescence, and so will you.

6. Becoming a Woman

You are experiencing or are about to experience a miracle called "puberty." Puberty is the time during adolescence when you are mature enough physically to become a mother. Those parts of your body that work together to make a baby are getting ready. If you have not already seen signs that the system is working, you soon will.

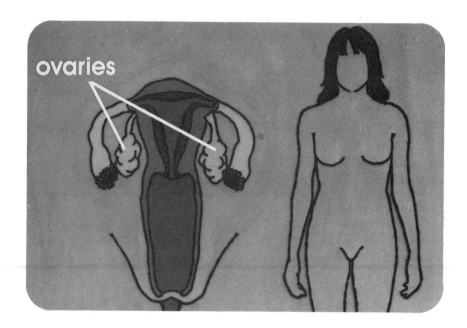

ovaries

The physical indication that a girl has become a woman begins with the ovaries, the female organs of reproduction located near the center of the body. When the ovaries mature, they begin to develop egg cells smaller than a pin point. Once this happens, one egg cell or ovum is released from the ovaries about every 28 days. This is called ovulation.

From the ovaries each tiny egg moves to the nearby fallopian (fa-LOW-pee-an) tube which leads to the uterus (YOU-ter-us) or womb. Fertilization occurs in the tube. The fertilized egg arrives in the uterus in about four days. In the uterus the ovum, if it has been fertilized by a male cell, will grow to become a baby.

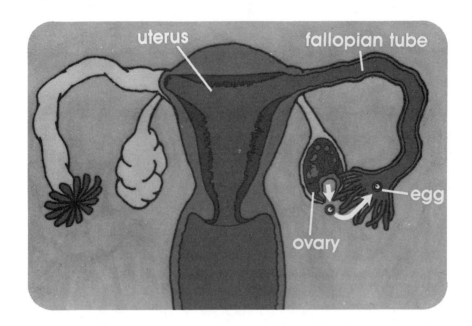

The uterus is a thick-walled, stretchy, hollow organ, about the size and shape of a fist. It can expand, like a balloon, to hold a growing baby. At the lower end of the uterus is the cervix (SER-viks). The cervix opens into the vagina (va-JY-na), the passageway from the uterus to the outside of the body.

The outside opening of the vagina is between the legs, where it is covered by folds of skin called the vulva (VUL-va).

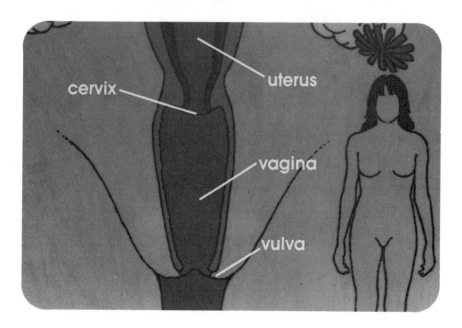

At the top of the vulva, where the inner folds of skin meet, is the clitoris (KLIT-or-is), a rounded tip of flesh the size of a pea. The clitoris has no part in creating life, but it is sensitive to touch and provides sexual pleasure for the woman.

The outside opening of the vagina in most girls is covered by the hymen (HI-men), a thin membrane. This opening lies between two other openings in the woman's body. In front is the urethra (u-REETH-ra), from which urine leaves the body, and in back is the anus (A-nus), from which solid waste leaves the body by way of the large intestine.

Egg cells, which leave the ovaries and are not fertilized, soon break up and pass from the walls of the uterus through the vagina as a combination of waste blood and tissue. This occurs about two weeks after they leave the ovaries. The process is called menstruation (men-stru-A-shun). For most girls this first happens when they are 12 or 13, but some begin to menstruate as early as 9 or as late as 16. Since the body has a regular period in which this occurs, menstruation is commonly called a woman's "period." The normal period lasts from 3 to 5 days and occurs approximately every 28 days. The first periods are likely to be irregular and even skip a month or two before a regular cycle is established.

Menstruation is not a sickness, and certainly it should not be thought of as the "woman's curse." It is the regular reminder that your body is ready for motherhood when you, your husband, and God decide it is time for fertilization to occur.

Some discomfort may occur during menstruation, but most women feel okay and continue their normal schedules and routines during that time. If you do experience cramps or aching in the lower back, especially at the beginning of your period, and if the pain or discomfort seems unusual, talk to your parents or to your doctor about it.

To protect your clothing during menstruation, some of you will use comfortable, convenient, sanitary pads or napkins available in various sizes and thicknesses. Others of you may prefer tampons, little rolls of absorbent material that are inserted into the vagina. Consult your mother, a school nurse, or a doctor if you have any questions about which to use.

After the menstrual period is over, the process repeats itself. Another egg cell matures and is released about two weeks after menstruation, when the follicle (the larger cell mass sheltering the growing egg) ripens. If the egg is not fertilized, menstruation again occurs. The whole series of events is called the menstrual cycle and normally repeats itself, except during pregnancy, about every 28 days until a woman is 45 to 55 years old, when her ovaries no longer release egg cells.

Although questions about ovulation, fertilization, and menstruation are perhaps the most common that girls your age ask, you may have others that deal with the development and maturing of your body. Perhaps you are concerned that your breasts don't seem to be developing as quickly or as fully as those of other girls your age. Or that they are developing too quickly or too fully. You may think it would be convenient if patterns were more consistent, that all girls' breasts started developing at exactly 11 years, for example, but that is not the way that God decided your body ought to work. You have your own personal "growth pattern" or clock. You can be sure that you will develop just at the rate God intends for your body. That may be earlier or later than any of your friends. It will happen, and it is normal to be different.

These are the signs mentioned earlier that tell how you're maturing:

Your hips start to broaden;

Your breasts may begin developing (and it's not unusual for one breast to grow more rapidly than the other);

Your pubic hair begins growing (this usually occurs before

menstruation and will appear in many variations of shape and amount);

You may notice a clear, whitish discharge from your vagina;

And you're growing quickly.

There you have it. It's not so awful, is it? Maybe a bit awe-filled. That's a big difference. You are wonderfully made; you have been given a wonderful gift and given the responsibility to treat it properly and respect it as a gift. Someday you may bear a child, maybe many children; or perhaps you will never have children. But whether or not you bear children doesn't change the fact of the gift or the wonder of it. *You* are the ultimate gift, complete, normal, special, important, and made in the image of God Himself. You are becoming a woman, someone who lives and breathes and loves and gives, whether you are alone or with others.

7. Becoming a Man

Boys may be different from girls, but they have just as many questions. The questions are slightly different, but they show many similar concerns about sex. Look at your list of questions from Chapter 1 and see whether any of these common ones are on your list:

"What size should a penis be?"

"Is it wrong to have 'wet dreams'?"

"What makes me feel the way I do about sex?"

Questions like these are normal, natural, and necessary. You have reached or soon will enter puberty, the time that your body tells you that you have become a man and are physically capable of being a father.

There is less consistency as to when you will reach puberty than there is with girls. One 14-year-old may not yet have any sign of hair on his face while another the same age might be 6'2" tall and wearing a beard. A foot difference in height between boys this age is not all that unusual. Boys usually reach puberty between 13 and 16, a year or two after girls. *This fact helps explain why girls are usually far more interested in dating during junior high than are boys.* But the time will come when you catch up, and it will come soon.

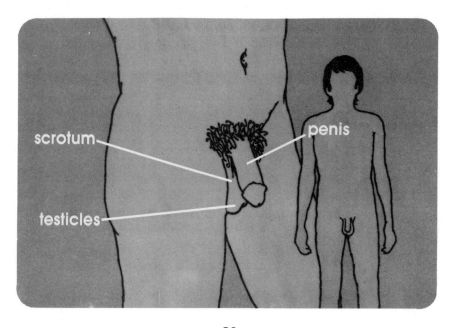

Although the man's reproductive system is less complicated than a woman's and doesn't run by a calendar, it is no less miraculous and no less interesting. The two most important parts of the man's reproductive system are the testicles (TESS-ti-kals) and the penis (PEE-nis). The testicles produce the sperm, the male cell that fertilizes the female egg. They also produce the hormone that causes boys' voices to become lower and hair to develop on their bodies at puberty. The two testicles hang behind the penis in a bag called the scrotum (SCRO-tum), and at full development they are about the size of a small egg.

In order to produce sperm cells, the testicles must have a temperature that is a little lower than the temperature inside the body. Also, the temperature must be kept constant or else the sperm cells already produced will die. How did God design the scrotum and testicles to take care of these needs?

First of all, by locating the testicles *outside* the body. Then, by designing the scrotum so that it automatically contracts and draws the testicles closer to the body when the outside temperature grows colder. When the body overheats, the scrotum relaxes so that the testicles may be farther from the warm pelvis. Finally, in order that the testicles do not injure each other when body movement brings the legs close together, God designed one testicle to hang lower in the scrotum than the other.

What a miracle of God the scrotum and testicles are!

The penis hangs between the legs, in front of the testicles. It is made up of spongy tissue filled with large blood vessels. The average penis is 3 to 4 inches in length when it is limp, but penis size varies greatly from person to person. The size of the penis has nothing to do with a man's ability to have sexual intercourse or to become a father.

At birth the end of the penis is partly covered by a loose skin called the foreskin. Many boys have this skin removed, usually just after birth, by a simple operation called "circumcision" (sur-kum-SIZH-un). The reason for circumcision may be medical—the foreskin is too tight; or hygienic—it's easier to keep a circumcised penis clean.

In Old Testament times God commanded Abraham and his descendants to circumcise their male children eight days after they were born. This religious ceremony was a sign of the special relationship between God and His Old Testament people.

Through the center of the penis runs the urethra (u-REETH-ra), the tube through which both sperm cells and urine leave the body. The urethra continues inside the body, extending to the bladder, where urine is stored.

If both sperm and urine pass through the urethra, do they come out at the same time? No. God has provided a wonderful mechanism to keep the sperm and urine separate. A valve at the

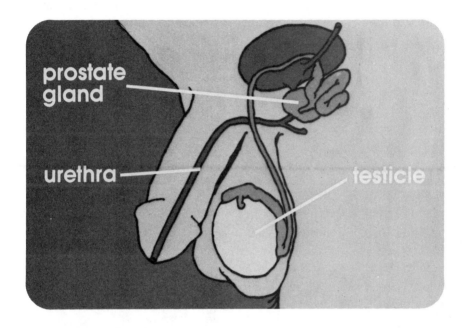

upper end of the urethra opens to let the urine pass out. This same valve closes tight, keeping the urine in the bladder, when sperm pass through the urethra.

The sperm, then, move from each testicle, where they are produced, up through a thin tube inside the body. These tubes (one from each testicle) are connected with the prostate gland at the base of the bladder. The prostate gland produces a whitish fluid in which the sperm cells swim. The sperm cells and this fluid together are called semen (SEE-men).

An erection of the penis occurs when the blood vessels in the penis expand to bring more blood into the penis. Valves in the vessels keep this blood under pressure, causing the spongy walls of the penis to expand and become hard. Even babies and young boys experience erections (e-REK-shuns), but they are common after a boy reaches puberty.

Sometimes erections occur from physical reasons, such as the need to urinate. Even tight clothes can cause an erection. The most common cause, though, is sexual excitement. Movement of or pressure on the erect penis, such as happens during sexual intercourse, will eventually result in an ejaculation (e-jak-you-LAY-shun), the release of semen from the penis in a series of throbbing spurts. The amount of this white, sticky fluid is one to three teaspoonsful. But even though sperm cells are only a small part of the fluid, one ejaculation can contain as many

as 400 million cells, each capable of fertilizing the single female egg.

Sometimes at night young men experience an ejaculation and wake up worried and upset. This is called a "nocturnal emission" or "wet dream," and it is perfectly normal. It is simply the body getting rid of excess semen. It first happens to most boys when they are 13 to 16 years old. Some young men have a lot of nocturnal emissions, some have few. The experience is natural and should not be thought of as abnormal or harmful.

You have a wonderful body, and the more you find out about it the more you will appreciate what God has given you. Like a woman, you have the potential to start new life. It is a great gift and an awesome one, for with fatherhood comes a great responsibility along with the pride.

Whether you do have children will depend on you, on your wife, and on God, but being a father is only one part of being a man. More important is how you use or control the fact that you are a man in your relationships with others. You yourself are a gift of God; He made you what you are to be a blessing to others and to Him. It's a challenge and an opportunity to be a man.

8. *The Miracle of Birth*

"So God created man in His own image, in the image of God He created him; male and female He created them. And God blessed them, and God said to them, 'Be fruitful and multiply, and fill the earth' " (Genesis 1:27-28).

These words from Genesis show how God made the man and the woman for each other. He wanted them to be happy together, and He wanted them to use their bodies to produce the children that would some day fill the earth. For this reason He made men and women different, and He made those differences something that would cause the man and the woman to be attracted to each other. Today we might call this "sex appeal" or "sexual attraction," but whatever it is called, it is a gift of God. Men and women are made in a way and with feelings that cause them to want to be together.

As you grow older, you will feel this attraction more and more. You will want to be with people of the other sex—in groups and with one person. As you grow older, you will want to date more often. You may well begin to date one special person.

As you get to know each other, you may fall in love and begin to look forward to marriage.

Marriage is God's plan for having babies—and for giving babies a mother and father who will love them and care for them. That's why God wants only married people to engage in this close, intimate, and loving relationship, known as sexual intercourse, the way babies begin. **"A man leaves his father and mother,"** the family where he grew up, **"and is united to his wife, and the two become one flesh" (Genesis 2:24 NEB).** They start a *new* family, in which a new father and mother can, in love, give birth to children and love and take care of their children.

Sexual intercourse is a very special part of marriage. It's a very special way in which a husband and wife show their love for each other. When a husband and wife are feeling close and loving, they find a private place to be together—usually their bedroom. They kiss and caress each other. Gradually they become ready for intercourse. In sexual intercourse, the husband's erect penis is put into the wife's moist vagina. The penis ejaculates semen into the wife's vagina. Both usually feel pleasure during sexual intercourse and feel relaxed and satisfied afterwards. Soon after ejaculation the penis again becomes limp.

If the woman has recently produced an egg cell, she can become pregnant. The man's sperm meet the egg cell. When one sperm enters the egg cell, that cell becomes "fertilized"—that is, no other sperm cell can now enter it, and that cell—the fertilized cell—is the beginning of a new human being. The fertilized egg gradually moves into the uterus, attaches itself to the wall of the uterus, and begins to grow. At this moment it is smaller than a pinpoint; and until the end of the second month it is called an embryo (EM-bree-oh). After that, until the baby is born, the growing child is called a fetus (FEE-tus).

Since extra blood is needed to nourish the growing egg as it develops into a baby, ovulation and menstruation do not occur while a woman is pregnant. The missing of a period is one way a woman senses she might be pregnant and is a reason for her to visit her doctor for an examination or tests that will make sure. If the woman is pregnant, the doctor will instruct her on the best way to care for her body in order to give her baby the best chance to develop normally.

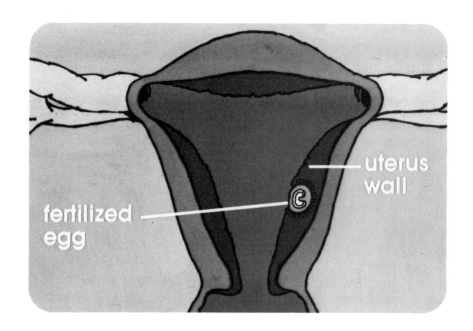

fertilized egg

uterus wall

About nine months after the egg and the sperm joined, the baby will be ready to be born. For several months mother and father have been able to feel the "kicks" of their baby in the mother's womb. Shortly before birth, the fetus usually turns in

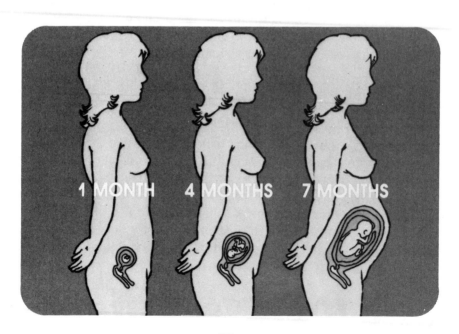

1 MONTH   4 MONTHS   7 MONTHS

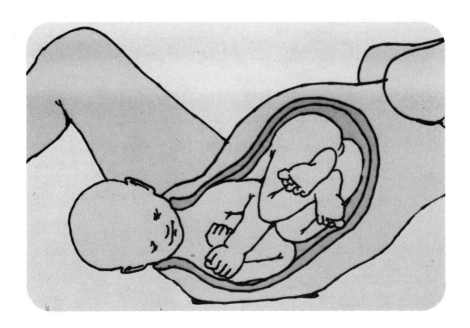

such a way that its head is pointed downward in the uterus. Then the muscles of the uterus, which have stretched to make room for the growing baby, begin to tighten and push, forcing the baby from the uterus into the vagina.

When this process called "labor" begins, the mother knows the birth will come soon and usually goes to the hospital so that a doctor can help with the delivery. The baby usually arrives in the world headfirst from the vagina, and with a gentle slap from the doctor soon gives out its first cry, a sure sign that it is breathing on its own. The umbilical (um-BIL-i-cul) cord, which joined the mother and baby in the womb and through which the baby received all its nourishment for nine months, is cut, leaving the navel or "belly button" on the baby's stomach.

Following the baby's birth, the placenta (pla-SEN-ta) or "afterbirth" leaves the mother's body through the vagina. The placenta is the mass of blood vessels that grew in the uterus to help provide nourishment for the baby. God's miracle of conception and birth is now complete!

Soon after birth, the mother's uterus returns to its usual size, and her breasts grow larger and begin to produce milk if she breast-feeds her new baby. If she chooses to bottle-feed her child, her breasts stop producing milk and return to their normal size.

Sometimes the embryo or fetus does not develop normally because of disease, injury, or some other problem. When this occurs and the baby is unable to survive or develop properly in the mother's uterus, her body rejects the dead fetus and pushes it from the body in a process called a miscarriage.

"It Looks Just Like You!"

Who in your family do you look like? Maybe you have your father's eyes or your mother's hair texture. Maybe you don't look very much like either of them. Regardless, both your father and your mother passed on to you a number of the features you have.

The sperm cell from the father contains 23 tiny elements called chromosomes. Each chromosome contains hundreds of parts called "genes" which determine what the child will look like. There are genes for the color of the skin, for the shape of the head, for body size—for all of the traits that describe how you look.

Similarly the egg cell of the mother contains 23 chromosomes, each with hundreds of genes. When the father's sperm cell unites with, or fertilizes, the mother's ovum or egg cell, the fertilized cell has 46 chromosomes that determine what the new baby will look like—half of them from the mother and half from the father.

Each of the father's 23 chromosomes is matched or fitted with the same chromosome of the mother. The genes, which are the actual carriers of the features, may be either "dominant" or "recessive." Dominant genes are stronger than recessive ones, which helps explain why blue-eyed parents can have brown-eyed children or dark-haired parents can have a blond child.

Remember, too, that both the mother and father received their chromosomes from their parents, and they from their parents. So each newborn baby receives a good mix of characteristics from many different ancestors. That's why you may have brown eyes, like your grandfather, rather than blue eyes like your mother's or gray eyes like your dad's.

What decided whether you're a boy or a girl? The sperm cell of the father. There are two kinds of sperm cells. One kind has what is called an X chromosome; the other, a Y chromosome. If an X chromosome fertilizes the ovum, the baby will be a girl. If a sperm with a Y chromosome fertilizes the egg cell, the baby will be a boy.

The more we study the wonders of conception and birth, the more we will agree with the psalm: "I am wonderfully made!"

9. *Men and Women Are Different, Aren't They?*

John: "What's a nice girl like you doing in a place like this?"

Mary: "C'mon, John, you know that baseball diamonds weren't made only for men!"

John: "Well, I don't know. 'A place for everything and everything in its place' is the way I see it."

Mary: "Fine, as long as you let me choose my place."

John: "Have it your way; I don't have time to argue. I've got to get to cheerleading practice. See you."

Sure, men and women are different. Recent studies by psychologists show that there are differences even between very young boy babies and girl babies. For example, girl babies respond sooner than do boy babies to the voices and faces of their parents. Boy babies are more likely to notice nearby objects. On the average, adult men see better than women in daytime, but women see better at night. But these and many other differences are *average* differences. They won't predict, too often, whether

Tom or Mary can see better in daytime. Nor are the inborn differences between the sexes very great.

Many differences between males and females develop because boys and girls were *treated* differently. They were expected to *be* different. For example, how often have you heard someone tell someone else—maybe you—to "act like a man" or to "act like a woman." What did that mean to you? Obviously you would have concluded that whatever you were doing at that moment was improper for your sex. And that kind of training goes a long way in setting in your mind some of the ideas you might be carrying now. Things like the following:

Men are more responsible than women.
Women like to be told what to do.
Men are more independent and need their freedom.
Women handle money and budgets better than men.
Men are strong and should never cry.
Women are sentimental and more gentle than men.
Men are better business managers or employers than women.
Women are better secretaries, cooks, teachers, and parents.
Men shouldn't do housework.
Women shouldn't do automobile repairs.
Etc., etc., etc.

The trouble is, when we say *all* women and *all* men are or have to be a certain way, we may keep some individuals from using the good gifts and talents God has given them. For example:

—Karen is a 14-year-old super athlete but is having trouble getting on a baseball team.

—Harold enjoys cooking, but his parents think that is a "girl's job."

—Shirley is a whiz at working on her dad's car. Some neighbors don't think that hobby is very "ladylike."

Do some investigating:

1. Does your family or your school treat males and females differently? In what ways?

2. Where else do you notice a different treatment of men and women?

3. Do you treat men and women differently? In what ways?

Discuss the differences you find with your parents or your

41

teachers. Are the differences in treatment helpful or harmful to individual males or females?

Also take time this week to watch television, looking specifically for impressions television might be making on viewers about male and female roles. Answer the following questions on the basis of your viewing:

1. How do the advertisements picture men? women?

2. If your local news program includes at least one woman, is she more likely to handle the news, the weather, or the sports?

3. Did you see any programs aimed at changing the typical views about men and women?

Take some time to compare your answers with those of your friends. And then talk about your thoughts on the subject, but make sure to include at least one person from the other sex in your conversation!

God created men and women different, but the differences were designed to bring them together, not to separate them. And the physical differences were not meant to set a limit on things that are not physical. A woman might not be able to throw a bale of hay as well as most men, but that doesn't mean she can't drive a tractor or manage a farm as well as or better than many men. A man might not have spent as much time in a kitchen as a woman while they were growing up, but that hardly means he is incapable of washing the dishes, doing the laundry, or planning and preparing a seven-course dinner.

Saying something isn't "man's work" or "woman's work" could be an excuse! In a family, a man's work and a woman's work are whatever needs to be done and can be done by the person with the time to do it.

In school, it's okay for boys to take home economics courses and for girls to take courses in shop or auto mechanics—if they want to, and if God has given them the talents. There's nothing wrong with "traditional" roles either, as long as they allow men and women to use their gifts wisely.

God has given all people gifts of all kinds to use in His service and the service of others. The question is: What gifts has God given *you*—and how will you use them?

You will be deciding in the next few years how you want to spend your life. Be yourself! Honestly examine your interests and your abilities. Be proud that you are a man or a woman, and look for ways to use what you are as fully as God intended in a way that gives credit to Him, to your sex, and to you. That was God's idea. Now take it and use it!

10. Getting Along with Friends

John: "Hey, Mary, you have lots of friends, don't you?"

Mary: "Yeah, I guess so. Why do you ask?"

John: "I don't have very many. I mean, I wait and wait and almost nobody comes to me wanting to be my friend."

Mary: "Well, you can't just sit and wait for friends to happen!"

John: "What do you mean?"

Mary: "Like they say, John, you've got to *be* a friend to have friends."

A song from the past said, "People who need people are the luckiest people in the world." The Christian poet John Donne wrote, "No man is an island," and that's surely true about women too. Almost everyone wants to be with other people, to be liked, to be needed, to be included in groups and clubs and teams. Only a few hermits claim not to need friends, and since you're probably not planning on taking "pre-hermit" classes, you'll want to have friends too.

And that's God's plan. He made people to live with and to share with other people. That's what the church is—God's people living with and helping and loving one another.

If you marry some day, you will have a special person to live with and to relate to, and sex will be an important part of that relationship. But another part of being a man or a woman is having friendships—close relationships with others—where sex is not a part. Both are perfectly natural and healthy.

You and Your Friends

Being a friend and having friends is a very important part of life. Especially during your teenage years, it is important to like yourself and to be with others who like themselves. If you don't like yourself, it's pretty hard for you to really like others and for them to think much of you. Even Jesus said to love your neighbor like you love yourself. After all, who wants to be around people who can't do anything but run themselves down? Liking yourself, then, is part of being a good friend.

What else makes a person a good friend? Look at the following list and see how these qualities fit your definition of a good friend.

A friend:

Is understanding,
Listens,
Is pleasant to be around,
Can be trusted,
Can be counted on,
Is open,
Is helpful,

Has similar interests,
Is considerate,
Is courteous,
Has a good sense of humor,
Has good manners,
Is easy to talk to.

Are there other things you'd add to the definition? Are some of these things unimportant to you? One way to check out how friendly you are and a way to work at becoming more friendly is to use this list to examine yourself and to practice doing some of those things that you might not have been doing in your relationships with others. Being friendly to others will always be one of the best ways to get and to keep friends.

Friendships are helpful in developing the values that guide what you do. You may notice that some of the things you do are modeled directly after actions of your friends. Perhaps you have noticed that you often talk like your friends, dress in similar ways, and do the same kinds of things. This is called "peer pressure," or pressure from those your age, and it will be an important force in your life. No one wants to be too different; looking like your friends and doing what they do is an important part of feeling accepted and belonging.

Most of the time this is fine, especially if the people who are your friends hold values and moral standards similar to yours. If you feel the constant pull from your friends to do things or say things that are different from the things that you believe are right, you are likely to create tension for yourself and for your relationship with your family.

At the same time you cannot always avoid contact with those people who live differently from you. In fact, you can be a Christian example. You can share the Good News of God's love and forgiveness even with those who laugh at you for being a Christian.

Someone once said that you can never have too many friends. That person was surely right, and you should be looking for ways to reach out and broaden your circle of friends. Too close an association with too small a group of friends is likely to stunt the growth of your personality.

At least you can make an effort to be friendly to everybody. A happy smile, a cheerful "hi"—even to strangers—can go a long way in helping people see you as a friendly person. It's pretty hard for anyone to ignore that kind of greeting, and it's a good way to get others to want to find out more about that person "who's always so friendly and cheerful."

The Dating Game

Even if you've never had a date, you've probably thought about dating. In the years ahead, the pressure to date and talk about dating are going to increase. So even if you're not particularly excited about dating, it won't hurt to think about it and to talk about the reasons teenagers want to and are expected to date. These are some of the more common reasons:

1. You don't want to be alone.
2. You need to feel accepted and worthwhile.
3. Dating makes you feel you're "with it."
4. You need to feel independent, to move out from family influence and be on your own.

5. You want a chance to try out adult behavior.

6. You want to have fun, and dating gives pleasure.

7. You want to develop close relationships with those of the other sex.

8. You want the special feeling that comes when someone cares enough for you to say "yes" to being with you.

No doubt you can add other reasons for wanting to date, but maybe your present thoughts about dating are more in the form of questions. Maybe you have some questions like these:

1. How old should I be before I start dating?

2. Is it wrong not to want to date yet?

3. How can I show my affection toward someone on a date without going "too far"?

4. How do I get a boy to ask me out?

5. What's the best way to ask a girl out?

6. What do I do on a date?

All of these are good questions, very normal ones for people your age. And when you ask them, you are going to find that lots of people are going to have answers for you. You will have some of your own answers, your friends will have some answers, and your parents and other adults are bound to want to get a few of their answers in too.

It's possible that your parents' answers will be different from your own. And that could cause conflict. Your parents will probably have some pretty set ideas about dating—even rules or at least guidelines for dating.

It may not seem like it at the time, but they're really thinking of you and your interests. God holds them responsible for bringing you up as a loving, responsible Christian person. And He calls on you to love, honor, and respect them. The best way to handle the conflicts that arise is to talk openly about differences without arguing. It may mean that the easiest solution will be to accept their rules, perhaps with the request that if you show you can meet their expectations that adjustments can be made to allow for the maturity you've shown.

"Everyone else can" may be true in many cases, but parents have heard it for years. It's probably more successful to ask for special permission to stay out late, for example, for a special occasion than to push for blanket approval of a time they aren't comfortable with. Each situation will be different, though, and the best way always is to work with each other in understanding and love.

The answers to most of the questions about dating can't be answered in some simple, standard way for everyone. God made you different from your friends, and your development will be different from theirs in many ways. You don't have to be like everyone else in the way you feel about dating, when you start dating, even in what you do on a date.

Remembering, then, that no definite, final answers about dating can apply to everyone, everywhere, let's try some tentative answers to the questions we asked earlier.

1. *How old should I be before I start dating?* Depends on what you mean by "dating." *Group*-dating is fine at any age. Group-dating is any fun activity with a group of boys and girls together—a party, a school social, a volleyball game at the beach, a softball game in the park, etc. No one is paired off with another specific person in a "group-date"—but boys and girls are getting to know each other better.

As you get to know what interests Kim or Terri or Elvis or John through a group date, you will be preparing yourself for a special kind of group date: Two or three boys ask two or three girls to a party at school, church, or in the neighborhood. This kind of "double-dating," in turn, will help you feel more confident, and will prepare you for single dating later.

Discuss with your parents whether you're ready yet for double dating—and, surely, for single dating, which most young people don't begin until the high school years.

2. *Is it wrong not to want to date yet?* Not at all! There's no rule about when to start dating. You don't have to prove anything to anyone by dating if you don't feel like it. But you'll want to spend time with larger groups of people, both boys and girls, doing things you like to do. Show your interest in others and in their interests. Let your own interests grow. And if special interests develop in one or more of the other sex, fine.

3. *How can I show my affection toward someone on a date without going "too far"?* Read what we say in Chapter 12, under "Sexual Experimentation." To summarize what we say there: Avoid trying to "make out" or "see what you can get out of" your date. As these slang phrases suggest, such an approach is selfish and self-centered. It conveys little respect for your date. Avoid situations that increase temptations. Pray for God's Spirit. Remember God's command—and the good reasons He has for restricting sexual intercourse to marriage. Remember how much Christ loves you and your date—and that He gave Himself up for you on the cross!

4. *How do I get a boy to ask me out?* For some occasions it's ok for you to ask *him* out! If, for example, you're giving a party or your school has a girl-ask-boy affair, simply ask the boy you'd like to be with. Be sure to ask early. And give him all the facts: when, where, what the date is all about.

If you want a boy to ask you out, be friendly to him whenever you see him. Show you're interested in him. Whenever you see him, encourage him to talk about his activities—hobbies, schoolwork, athletic events. Hard as it is, try not to be too pushy. Most boys shy away from a girl who tries to take charge or who quite obviously hints that she wants to be asked out.

5. *What's the best way to ask a girl out?* Come right out and ask—giving the time, the place, and the nature of the date: "May I take you to the class picnic at Babler Park next Friday? We could leave about 10 in the morning." This is a lot better than, "Whatcha doin' next Friday?" (This puts the girl down and makes it sound like you haven't planned anything interesting to do.) Even worse is: "I don't suppose you'd be interested in going out with me, would you?" (This puts *you* down. It suggests that she answer "no.")

6. *What do I do on a date?* Even when you're ready to date and want to, it's not always easy to start. You're nervous about asking, and you're nervous about accepting. You want to say and do just the right thing. Be yourself. Don't try to overdo but settle for the easy things—a movie, a concert, a party of some kind. Being with another couple or two or in a group lessens the chance for those moments of "nothing to say" and the temptations to go past those boundaries of proper action that you have set.

There will be times of doubt and disappointment, times of frustration and maybe even times bordering on despair. But the dating years are great years, years during which you become the person you will be for a long time. God had a good reason for making the years of physical growth and the years of social growth happen at the same time. When they're finished, you'll feel ready to be an adult. They won't last all that long; enjoy them right now!

11. *Getting Along with Family*

Mary: "John, do you like your family?"

John: "Sure. I mean, I guess so. But we do our share of arguing and fighting."

Mary: "So do we. But we still love each other!"

John: "We do, too. But I just wish we would listen more to each other."

Mary: "That's a big trouble with parents, I think. They just don't listen."

John: "That's what *my* parents say about *me!*"

You may have noticed that the amount of disagreement between you and others in your family has increased in the last couple of years. Such conflict certainly isn't pleasant, but it might help to realize that it's pretty common in most families. It doesn't automatically mean that your home is falling apart and that everyone is failing in their efforts to be a family. It probably does mean that both parents and children are adjusting to new roles. If everyone sees that it is part of development, these moments of conflict can teach both parents and children to understand and to better handle these new roles.

But it's not pleasant. You've already read about the problems that arise about matters of sex, about growing up, and about dating. And you surely can think of other areas where you or your friends have really run into trouble with parents. Whether you consider the things you argue about "big things" or "little things," one of the biggest causes of misunderstanding is the unwillingness of either side to really listen to what the other is saying. Parent and child feel so strongly about their position that they fail even to consider the possibility of another point of view.

Taking time to listen to the other person *will* help; so will stopping to ask why you're getting so upset. Is it really worth it? Why is it so important to you and to the other person? Instead of trying to decide who is right and who is wrong, a starting point based on love and understanding might help.

Obviously you're never going to be able to do everything your parents expect you to, even if you wanted to. And they'll disappoint you, too, in the way they talk or act. But God didn't bring you together to be a *perfect* family, but one willing to forgive and share and grow and learn together in love.

Sometimes parents really don't understand that you are capable of handling more responsibility; sometimes they simply expect too much. And perhaps you sometimes forget that your parents do most of what they do because they love you and want only what is best for you. Sometimes it's hard for parents to "let go of their little kid" whom they have raised and cared for in both good and bad times. Sometimes your growing up only means to them that they are growing old. Both sides can learn a lot about patience and understanding and sharing the love and forgiveness that God's love makes possible. His presence during all arguments can take away a lot of the sting.

All this understanding won't take away the areas of conflict. They will still be there. Parents may continue to remind you what they did or what they didn't have when they were young. They may try to shape you into something they wanted to be but didn't get to; maybe they'll push you toward a profession they like but you have no interest in.

And parents will continue to want a voice in your selection of friends—of either sex. But if you listen and try to understand what they are saying, you just may hear a little wisdom and a lot of love and understanding tucked around those words that seem to criticize everything you do. And sometimes, they might even be right!

Some of you may be growing up in a single-parent home, one in which either Mom or Dad is no longer present. The number of such homes is increasing and brings special needs and special opportunities for the teenager. Managing such a home is especially hard for the single parent, and they will expect you to carry more of the load and perhaps to grow up faster than in the two-parent home. But in spite of the absence of one of the most important models in your life, you receive the chance to experience firsthand the opportunities to be a helpful, absolutely necessary part of all the things parents do. It's not easy, but it's the kind of situation in which God has promised to supply a special measure of His Spirit.

Whatever your home environment, whether you live with one parent, two parents, foster parents and whether you have younger brothers and sisters who torment you or older brothers and sisters to whom you constantly get compared, your family is God's gift to you and you are God's gift to it. You'll have times when you'd like to give your family back, and probably there will be times when they'd like to give you back. But your family is God's plan, His design, and He is right there watching and helping those who invite Him in. It's an awfully good idea to send that invitation, especially at the time when the argument starts and before those words and actions occur that you'll wish later you could take back. He'll be there immediately.

12. Special Questions

Mary: "Well, I know a lot more than I did before."

John: "Yeah, me, too. But I still have more questions. Some of the things I worry about haven't even been mentioned."

Mary: "Oooh, you mean *you* think about some unmentionable things?"

John: "Ah, come on, Mary; you know what I mean."

Mary: "I'm just kidding. Believe me, I think about the same things."

John: "You do? No kidding ..."

The subject of sex raises lots of special questions, difficult questions that aren't easy to talk about and aren't easy to answer. This section will touch on some of the better-known problem subjects. If your own question isn't answered in this section, be sure to ask some adult you trust: your parents, your pastor, your teacher, or your guidance counselor.

Pornography

One of the growing forms of temptation that you will have to face is pornography (por-NOG-rah-fee), pictures and writing that make sex dirty. "Adult" bookstores, magazines, immoral pictures, X-rated movies, and live shows all picture the body as something to be used, abused, and lusted after rather than something to be thankful for, admired, and treated as the gift of God. Most of these books, pictures, and places claim to be "off limits" to those under 18 or 19 years of age. But even junior high students may still come into contact with pornography—even though they may not be looking for it. We live in a society that glamorizes sex, and bodies, through ads, movies, TV. It's all around us.

It will not be an easy temptation for you to ignore, but there are things you can do. You can remember always that your body and the bodies of others are the gifts of God. You can be aware that such pornographic materials exist, yet you can avoid them. You can avoid those situations that might pull you into groups whose actions and words degrade sex and the human body. And you can pray daily for strength to resist the pressure to "be one of the gang" or "be modern" or "join the world." (See Philippians 4:8.)

Masturbation

A majority of both boys and girls masturbate at some time in their lives. Masturbation is the handling or rubbing of the penis or clitoris to gain pleasure or until release of sexual pressure, or orgasm, is reached.

In years past, parents, teachers, and books told teenagers that masturbation would lead to blindness, to deafness, to loss of hair, even to sterility (the inability to have children), or insanity. None of these are true. Medical authorities agree that there are no harmful physical effects caused by masturbation.

Some authorities are concerned, though, that masturbation can turn into a kind of "self-love" that keeps young people from developing normal social relationships with others. While masturbating, a person often has lustful daydreams or impure thoughts. Later, there will be feelings of guilt and shame. These harmful effects of masturbation can't be ignored.

Here are some ways to overcome the habit of masturbation: Spend more time in activities with others—sports, clubs, hobbies—whatever interests you and will bring you into contact with people. Avoid pictures and books and conversations that are sexually stimulating. "Whatever is true ... whatever is pure, whatever is lovely ... think about these things," writes the apostle Paul (Philippians 4:8). In other words, replace impure thoughts with thoughts about all the exciting, interesting, beautiful things and people in God's world. Most of all, ask God for His strength and power to resist temptation. And remember that He keeps on loving you and forgiving you for Jesus' sake.

Sexual Experimentation

Maybe you've heard friends or schoolmates brag about "making out," about experiences with sex that no one else in the group has had. For many, these stories are like a game or contest. Each person wants to show that he or she knows more or has "done" more than anyone else in the group. Of course, these stories are often exaggerations—or even plain lies. But they can lead you to feel inferior, abnormal, or at least "out of it." They can cause you to experiment with sex to prove that you are a "real man" or a "real woman."

Certainly as you begin to date, you will find that you want to kiss, to hold, to touch the person you are with. Such activities are not wrong, but you will soon discover the need to draw some lines in your own mind about what is proper.

To do something just to see if you can "get away" with it or to see how far you can go degrades the person you are with. It can't lead to friendship or to real love. If you want to do something to prove your courage or so you can brag about it, you are wrong.

The best guideline seems to be drawing the line at those touches that might lead you and your partner beyond the point of control and into sexual intercourse. You will learn that the best guide is to be considerate of the other person; to avoid trying to do things that the other person is uncomfortable with. If you draw lines that you are comfortable with, and if you avoid situations that increase the chances of stepping beyond those lines, you will better enjoy your relationship. You will respect yourself and the person you are with. For example, don't get together in a house where no adults are home. Most teen pregnancies begin in someone's home.

Most of all, remember that as a Christian you can call on the power of God's Spirit. "If you are guided by the Spirit you will not fulfill the desires of your lower nature [your sinful self]. ... Anyone can see the kind of behavior that belongs to the lower nature: fornication [sexual intercourse between unmarried people], impurity, and indecency. ... But the harvest of the Spirit is love, joy ... self-control. ... If the Spirit is the source of our life, let the Spirit also direct our course" (Galatians 5:16–25 NEB).

Why is sexual intercourse sinful before marriage but "good" and even commanded after marriage? Because God planned intercourse as the highest expression of love between a husband and a wife. Sexual intercourse in marriage unites a husband and wife into "one flesh."

What's more, by restricting sexual intercourse to marriage, God strongly protects the helpless babies who are born as a result of sexual intercourse. Who best can care for a baby? Who will best love a baby? What does a baby need? A mother and a father, who love each other and are joined in a family to care for their children!

The Bible therefore warns against *fornication* and *adultery*. Fornication is sexual intercourse between unmarried people. Adultery is sexual intercourse by a married person with someone other than the wife or husband. In both these sins, the man or woman gives in to his or her own selfish desires and disregards God's Law.

Many people who give in to these sins, of course, claim that they can "love" the person they are having intercourse with even though they are not married to that person. But what kind of "love" is it that says, "My pleasure comes first"? "I don't care what God says—or what may happen if I hurt my wife or husband by having intercourse with someone else." That kind of "love" is really "lust."

When Jesus spoke, in Matthew 5:28, about a "lustful" look and "adultery" in the heart, He wasn't talking about our good, God-created interest in and attraction to people of the other sex. He meant the selfish misuse of that desire. Love cares about and cares for the other person. Lust uses the other person for its own pleasure.

"Husbands, love your wives, *as Christ loved the church and gave Himself up for her*" (Ephesians 5:25). Remember how Christ loved you! That's the way husbands, wives, and young people who are about to date can turn from lust and grow in love.

Birth Control

What is "birth control"? Any method that people who are having intercourse may use to prevent pregnancy. There are a number of birth control methods. Birth control *pills* taken regularly by a woman prevent ovulation by "tricking" the body into thinking pregnancy has taken place. Birth control *foam*, used by the woman, kills the sperm before they reach the egg.

Condoms or "rubbers" fit over the penis and prevent the sperm from entering the vagina. The *diaphragm* is a rubber cap that a woman inserts into her vagina to keep the sperm from getting into her uterus.

In natural methods of family planning, a woman closely keeps track of her monthly periods, avoiding intercourse during those times each month when she is most likely to get pregnant. This method is called the "rhythm" method.

Men and women may also be *sterilized* by having an operation that prevents pregnancy. On the man this is done by cutting the tubes that carry sperm from the testicles. On the woman, its done by tying shut the fallopian tubes. Both of these sterilization operations are ordinarily permanent. Once they're done, they can't be undone. They do not, however, affect the ability to have sexual intercourse.

Many Christians are concerned about the motives for practicing birth control, particularly if the couple is against children and the responsibilities that children bring. Also, some Christian churches permit only "natural methods" of birth control since they view other methods as being against God's will.

Birth control allows a married couple to plan more carefully when to have children and how many they will have. Because birth control methods are readily available and to a certain extent remove the fear of pregnancy, they have no doubt encouraged more and more unmarried people to have intercourse. So in recent years there have been *more* unmarried pregnancies than ever before. How come? Well, for one, many unmarried people simply don't bother to use any birth control methods. Then, too, none of the birth control methods is 100 percent effective.

Unmarried—and Pregnant

There are more birth control devices than ever before—and people can get them easier than ever before. Yet more and more unmarried girls are getting pregnant. At least 10 percent of all teenage girls become pregnant before marriage. Even in strong Christian homes there may be an unmarried pregnancy. Very likely, you know of boys and girls who are experiencing or who have experienced this very real problem. And it is a problem in which both boys and girls are equally involved—because it takes a boy to get a girl pregnant.

The young girl who becomes pregnant faces several decisions about what to do. She and the father of the child may decide to marry. If they do, they need to be aware of the difficulties they will face. For example, such a marriage has four times as great a chance of ending in divorce as do other marriages. And such a marriage can interrupt or stop them from finishing school and developing their abilities. Nevertheless, such a marriage can succeed if both father and mother are willing to make the necessary sacrifices. As they trust in God for forgiveness and for strength, they can grow in their love for one another.

The girl may also decide to have the baby and then to give it up for adoption. Many girls choose to do this, letting the baby be placed in a home that is able to provide for it and give it the love and security of strong parents who are delighted to have a child at last. A mother who makes the sacrifice of giving up her child—and the child who is adopted by loving parents—will find special meaning in this word from God: "God sent forth *His* Son, born of woman ... so that we might receive adoption as sons. And because you are sons, God has sent the Spirit of His Son into our hearts, crying, 'Abba! Father!' " (Galatians 4:4–6).

Numerous unmarried women who are pregnant are choosing to have an abortion—that is, to have the unborn embryo or fetus killed in their womb before it is born. But what a terrible sin this is! Only God has the right to give and take away life. Killing an embryo or fetus is nothing less than killing a human person,.

Some girls decide to have the baby and to keep it, perhaps with the aid of their parents. Such a decision will cause problems, to be sure. The mother may find it hard to take care of her baby and also continue going to school. It may be more difficult for her to get married later. But again, this advice can work out as the mother looks to the Father in heaven for the support and strength she will need.

In any case, all those involved in an unwanted pregnancy need the strong support and forgiving love of relatives and friends. Most of them recognize their sin and need to hear God's forgiveness in Christ. They need help, too, to seek out God's will

57

for their lives and for the baby who will be born.

Sexually-Transmitted Diseases

What are "sexually-transmitted diseases" (STDs)? Diseases you get from having intercourse with—or, sometimes, from kissing—an infected person. There are over 20 different and dangerous STDs. The most common are chlamydia (kla-MID-ee-ah), herpes (HER-pees), syphilis (SIF-i-lis), human papilloma (pap-i-LO-ma) virus (HPV), and gonorrhea (gon-ah-REE-ah). Doctors are learning more and more about how to cure these diseases, yet more and more people are getting them—especially people 13 to 22 years old. STDs infect three million teenagers annually.

The chlamydia bacterium (germ) infects the urethra in men and women, and may inflame or scar the sex organs so that the person becomes infertile. The herpes simplex virus (Type 2) causes itching and painful blisters on the genitals. Signs of syphilis first appear 10 to 90 days after infection as a chancre (Shang-ker) sore on or near the sex organs, but such sores don't always occur. HPV causes warts on both women's and men's genital organs and also cancer of the cervix. Symptoms are not always noticeable in gonorrhea, although infected men sometimes notice a whitish discharge from the penis three to eight days after infection. Women usually have no early signs that they have gonorrhea, but the later effects of the disease are as serious for them as they are for men.

Many sexually-transmitted diseases can be treated and cured by early diagnosis and medical treatment. But because the disease may not give an early warning sign, many people believe they don't have the disease and so they let it go untreated. If they aren't treated, chlamydia, syphilis, HPV, and gonorrhea are extremely serious. They can lead to blindness, heart trouble, infertility, cancer, and even death. Although herpes is not life-threatening for most people, there is no cure. Although genital warts can be treated, there is no cure for HPV. There are no vaccines for any of these diseases.

In 1981, doctors began to report a new disease called AIDS. AIDS is caused by a virus that can be passed from one person to another mostly by sexual contact or by sharing drug needles and syringes used for "shooting" drugs. The AIDS virus attacks a person's immune system and damages one's ability to fight other diseases. The body can then easily get all kinds of life-threatening diseases, such as pneumonia, meningitis, and cancer.

There is no cure for AIDS and no vaccine to prevent it.

Many young AIDS patients did not get the disease through sex. Some got it from infected, shared needles when "shooting" drugs. Others became infected through contaminated blood products. And some were born with it, because an infected mother can pass AIDS to her fetus, and later through her breast milk. Nevertheless, the great majority of AIDS patients got the disease from sexual contact. It can take up to six months to test positive for the HIV virus and then another 10–15 years for symptoms to begin.

Chlamydia, herpes, syphilis, HPV, and gonorrhea come only from sexual contact, and the only sure way to prevent them is to refrain from intercourse outside of marriage, and to stay faithful to one's spouse within marriage. If you ever have any fear that you might have such a disease, see a doctor immediately.

Homosexuality

Homosexuality means sexual attraction to those of the same sex. Homosexuals include men attracted to men and women attracted to women. Women homosexuals are also called "lesbians." There are many nicknames for homosexuals such as "gay," "fairies," "faggots," "fruits," "dykes," and "queers."

What makes some people homosexuals? No one knows for certain. But God's Word is clear that homosexual behavior is against God's will and is sinful.

Most of you will feel no temptation toward any sort of sexual relationship with someone of your own sex. It's normal to admire someone of the same sex, such as a good friend or an older person. This is not homosexual behavior.

Remember, too, that no one can identify homosexuals by the way they look. Often people are called homosexual for reasons based on hatred, suspicion, and ignorance, certainly not on fact. The reputation of some people has been seriously damaged because someone thought they didn't look "masculine" enough or "feminine" enough, and then suggested that they are homosexual. This is a cruel and common practice, and being aware of this fact can help you avoid this kind of unkindness.

You may have to make decisions about homosexuals, whether you will include them in your group, for example, and you may find it hard to separate fact from fiction at that time. In dealings with homosexuals you will find it helpful to remind yourself that Christ died and rose again for the forgiveness of homosexuals and heterosexuals alike. God says clearly what is wrong, and He says clearly that sin is forgiven in Christ. Both homosexuals and heterosexuals can be guilty of sinful lusts. All people are sinners and fail to obey God's Law. No one who asks for forgiveness is beyond receiving it fully.

You will need to show understanding and Christian love to homosexuals if you are to give them the strength to turn to God for forgiveness and to Christian counselors for help. Only the love of God in Jesus and the power He brings can give you the strength to reject temptation and to reach out in forgiveness and Christian love.

Guilt Feelings

Young people sometimes do things connected with sex or think about sex in a way that they know is wrong. They feel guilty and know that they have fallen short of their own standards, God's standards, and the standards others expect them to follow. The result can be some pretty bad moments spent criticizing themselves for what they've thought or done.

Guilt feelings about sex are fine as far as they go; they serve a purpose just like guilt feelings about other things you do wrong. You say something nasty to your parents, you cheat "just a little" on a test, you lie about something else, and you feel guilty. Sexual sins are no different from other sins in the eyes of God. They are wrong.

But the great thing about being a Christian is that God the Judge is also God the Lawyer in our behalf and the God of forgiveness. God the Father sent His Son to die for *all* your sins and all the sins of everybody else. With His resurrection came our forgiveness that wipes out all our sins and all our guilt about them. Feeling guilty makes you look for help. Thank God that Jesus brings help and forgiveness. Trust His Word to you: "I forgive you; go in peace!"

Jesus also said, "Sin no more." Well, you know you're going to sin again, but the forgiveness God gives also gives the power to live a new life, one aimed at trying to live more the way God wants. It also gives the power to confess, to apologize, and to forgive others when they do things to you that are wrong. And, above all, it gives the assurance that whenever you fall short of your own goals for living—and you will—the same forgiveness is waiting every time, just as full and just as total as the first time.

13. The New You

Mary: "It's been fun talking to you."

John: "It really was. You're a good friend, you know. Thank you for listening."

Mary: "I'd like to talk again sometime if that's all right with you."

John: "Anytime! Hey, would you like to go to the dance at school with me Friday night?"

Mary: "I'd love to. I thought you'd *never* ask!"

And just like that, you will continue to grow, physically and in your relationships with other people of both sexes, with your family, and with God. The days and months and years just ahead of you are bright and exciting and so full of chances to use what God has given you.

The frustrations and disappointments will not end, but the joys and blessings will far outnumber them. You've reached the end of this book but not the end of learning about yourself and about others. Take these few reminders with you as you go on from here:

1. Accept yourself as a real and worthwhile gift from God. Keep looking in that mirror and see what a special person you are.

2. Work at your friendships. Reach out and help others. Be thoughtful toward them and treat them the way you'd like to be treated.

3. Keep your body active and healthy. Take care of it since it's the only one you'll have. Eat wisely, take time for rest and recreation, develop your special interests, and *use* the gifts God has given you.

4. Improve your skills. Work at those areas in which you can achieve. Strengthen the weak spots. Decide to be the best you can be at whatever you try, accepting your strengths and your limits.

5. Share your thoughts and ideas with others. Talk to them. Ask for advice, and don't be afraid to risk being fair, just, and Christian. Open up to those you admire and trust. Be honest with your parents and friends.

6. Keep in touch with God. He's so close that you won't have to worry about getting His attention. Use regular church worship and Bible study as ways to grow in fellowship with God's people.

7. Accept your family, just the way they are. Work to talk and to listen better. Forgive them and expect them to forgive you. Show them your love with words and with a hug now and then.

8. Continue to share God's love with others. Tell others about what you believe; tell them God loves them. God has put you here for that purpose, too. Share the Good News any way you can.

9. Enjoy and celebrate life. Take your gift of sexuality eagerly and use it the way God intended. Enter your maturity with joy; accept its challenges with excitement. Forgive as you have been forgiven. Practice "save sex until marriage" instead of "safe sex." There is no such thing as "safe sex" outside of marriage.

10. Remember that you are an important person—right now! God is with you and cares for you today. You are His and He's not about to let you go. Give a shout of joy, lift your head high, and walk with confidence into the life that's waiting.

14. Word List

Abortion (a-BOR-shun) Ending a pregnancy by killing the embryo or fetus.

Abstinence (AB-stin-ens) To refrain from sexual intercourse.

Acne (ACK-nee) Pimples and blackheads on the face and other parts of the body.

Adolescence (ad-uh-LESS-ens) The period of life between childhood and adulthood. The teen years.

AIDS See Sexually Transmitted Disease.

Circumcision (ser-kum-SIZH-un) An operation that removes the foreskin from the end of the penis.

Clitoris (KLIT-o-ris) A small organ at the front of the vaginal opening which gives sexual pleasure when touched.

Conceive (kon-SEEV) To start a new life through union of a sperm cell with an egg cell; to become pregnant.

Condom (KON-dom) A thin rubber sheath placed over the erect penis before intercourse to prevent sperm from entering the vagina. Because of its high rate of failure, it does not provide a "safe sex" prevention of STDs, as is often claimed.

Ejaculation (e-jac-u-LAY-shun) The discharge of semen from the penis.

Embryo (EM-bree-oh) The unborn baby during the first eight weeks after conception.

Erection (e-REC-shun) The enlarging and hardening of a male's penis during sexual excitement.

Fallopian Tubes (fa-LOW-pee-an) The passageway connecting the ovaries to the uterus. The fertilizing of the egg by the sperm normally takes place here.

Fetus (FEE-tus) The unborn baby after eight weeks or more in the mother's uterus.

Genital (JEN-i-tal) Pertaining to the sex organs.

Homosexuals (hoh-moh-SEK-shoo-als) Men and women who prefer to satisfy their sexual desires with members of their own sex.

Intercourse (IN-ter-corse) The sexual union of a male and female; the inserting of the penis into the vagina.

Masturbation (mass-ter-BAY-shun) Sexual stimulation by handling or rubbing the genital organs.

Menopause (MEN-o-pauz) The time in life when the ovaries stop ovulating. Conception is no longer possible.

Menstruation (men-stroo-AY-shun) The monthly flow of waste blood and tissue from the uterus. It is commonly called a "period."

Navel (NAY-vel) The depression in the middle of the stomach where the umbilical cord was connected.

Nocturnal Emission (nok-TER-nal ee-MISH-un) The release of semen during sleep, common in adolescent boys. Also called a "wet dream."

Orgasm (OR-gaz-um) A series of pleasurable muscular contractions centered in the sexual organs and affecting the entire body.

Ovary (OH-va-ree) The female reproductive organ in which egg cells develop and sex hormones are produced.

Penis (PEE-niss) The male sex organ that hangs between the legs and through which both urine and semen pass out of the body.

Pituitary (pih-TYOO-i-ter-ee) The body's master gland located at the base of the brain. Its secretions control and regulate many organs and influence most basic body functions.

Pornography (por-NOG-ref-ee) Books, movies, or videos that make sex dirty without a concern for God's Word or moral values.

Prostate Gland (PROS-tate GLAND) A male gland which secretes fluid that mixes with sperm.

Puberty (PYOO-ber-tee) The time of becoming mature and being capable of reproducing. This usually occurs between ages 13 and 16 in boys and 11 and 14 in girls.

Safe Sex The false idea that intercourse with appropriate "safeguards" such as condoms will keep people from getting an STD. The only safe sex is with an uninfected partner in a marriage where husband and wife are faithful to each other.

Scrotum (SKROH-tum) A bag of skin which hangs from the groin between the legs of a male. It supports and protects the testicles.

Semen (SEE-men) The male fertilizing fluid that is made up of sperm and the whitish liquid in which they flow.

Sexual Abuse Being touched inappropriately by an adult or peer. (It's important to tell someone right away when abuse happens to you or someone you know.)

Sexually Transmitted Disease (STD) Any of a variety of contagious diseases contracted almost entirely from sexual contact. The most common are AIDS, chlamydia, herpes, syphilis, human papilloma virus (HPV), and gonorrhea.

Sperm (SPERM) The male cell produced in the testicles to fertilize the female egg.

Sterile (STEHR-il) Being unable to produce babies.

Testicles (TESS-ti-kals) The two egg-shaped male reproductive glands where sperm are produced.

Urethra (u-REETH-ra) The tube through which urine passes from the bladder out of the body. In males it also carries the semen.

Uterus (YOO-ter-us) Also called the womb. The place where the fertilized egg develops into a fully formed baby.

Vagina (vah-JY-na) The passageway leading from the vulva to the uterus in a woman; the birth canal.

Virgin (VER-jin) A person who has never had sexual intercourse.

Vulva (VUL-va) The external female sex organs surrounding the genital opening.